PLAY BETTER GOLF

PERFECTING YOUR SHORT GAME

Saving shots around the green

Beverly Lewis

Illustrations by Ken Lewis

SMITHMARK

CLB 3149
© 1991 CLB Publishing,

This edition published in 1994 by
SMITHMARK Publishers, Inc.,
16 East 32nd Street, New York, NY 10016

SMITHMARK books are available for bulk purchase for sales
promotion and premium use. For details write or call the
manager of special sales, SMITHMARK Publishers, Inc.,
16 East 32nd Street, New York, NY 10016; (212) 532-6600.

Produced by CLB Publishing,
Godalming Business Centre, Woolsack Way,
Godalming, Surrey GU7 1XW

ISBN 0-8317-4034-5

Printed and bound in Malaysia
10 9 8 7 6 5 4 3 2 1

Contents

Beverly and Ken Lewis

Beverly Lewis became a professional golfer in 1978 and has twice been Chairman of the Women's Professional Golf Association. A PGA qualified professional since 1982, she has played in many major tournaments and is an experienced teacher. She has been a regular contributor to *Golf World* magazine in the United Kingdom for six years and is the only woman on their teaching panel. She has won two tournaments on the WPGA circuit but now concentrates on her teaching commitments.

Beverly is co-author of *Improve Your Golf* (published in the UK by Collins Willow, revised edition), and has written the other titles in the *Golf Clinic Series*. Her interests include music and playing the organ.

Ken Lewis trained at the Southend College of Art and then worked as a commercial artist. He has illustrated many golf books, working with players such as Peter Alliss, Alex Hay and Sandy Lyle. His projects include illustrating newspaper instructional features and strips by Greg Norman and Nick Faldo, and he works for *Golf* Magazine in the United States. His hobbies include building and flying his own aeroplane.

CHAPTER ONE

Putting – so easy yet so hard

I can remember that during one family holiday, we went to the putting green on the seafront and proceeded to have a competition. I had been playing golf for some three or four years, and had a fairly good idea of what I was supposed to be doing. But did I win? Beaten by non-golfers, I don't think I even came a poor third. I was so overcome by the inadequate conditions and equipment with which I was playing that I completely forgot what I was trying to achieve.

So what are you aiming to achieve when you are putting? Ideally, you are setting the ball rolling on a predetermined line, which will result in the ball going in the hole. Obviously, there are times when you know that you will be lucky just to get the ball near to the hole, but even then, you must concentrate on making the best stroke possible. In my seafront disaster, I took one look at the surface of the putting green, and the putter in my hand, decided that there was no way to ever get the ball near the hole, and then proceeded to confirm my negative ideas by putting appallingly. I had lived up to my own expectations of what I thought was or was not possible, and in that one instance learnt that confidence was so important.

Of course, confidence is always essential in golf, but when it comes to putting – the simplest of movements that even the rawest beginner can develop a halfway decent putting stroke very quickly – is of the utmost importance if you are to capitalize on your ability.

I have given many putting clinics during golf tuition

weeks, and I know that most pupils feel that their time would be better spent on perfecting their driving skills. However, they often come back to me later in the week having played under their handicap, simply because, for the first time in their lives, they had a good idea of what they were trying to do on the putting green, and had therefore eliminated three and four putting to a large degree.

Nothing is more galling than to outplay an opponent from tee to green, only to see him or her, time and again, slot the most impossible of putts. You may regard this as an injustice, and so often your frustration at being beaten by a superior putter, rather than a superior golfer, detracts from your concentration on the game, and thus you go from bad to worse.

Since there is so little movement involved in a putt, we are quite capable of incorporating unwanted adjustments at any time throughout the stroke. Unlike the full swing, in which, once you have started the downswing, the sheer momentum takes over to a great extent, in a putt you have little momentum and consequently can turn the putter blade out of line quite easily.

Good putters only see and feel positive things, and on good days they know that they will hole many putts. However, confidence alone will not overcome poor technique, so first you must learn the correct basic fundamentals, such as grip and set up, before you even consider the stroke.

CHAPTER 2

The grip

I have seen a wide range of weird and wonderful ways of gripping the putter, which seem to work for their owners, but as a teacher I would never recommend them to anyone. Today's best putters all tend to grip the club in a similar fashion, which has evolved over the years, so among professionals you are less likely to see many grips that vary significantly from the norm.

When putting, try to place your hands on the grip so that the palm of the right, and back of the left are parallel to the club face. This enables you to relate very easily to the position of the club face during the stroke and, more importantly, at impact. With your hands in this position, both thumbs will sit on top of the grip. Incidentally, I would recommend that you have a putter grip on the club, rather than just an ordinary golf grip. The putter grip has a flattened front, which assists considerably in obtaining the

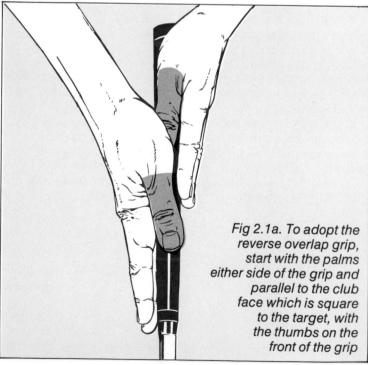

Fig 2.1a. To adopt the reverse overlap grip, start with the palms either side of the grip and parallel to the club face which is square to the target, with the thumbs on the front of the grip

correct grip every time, and also helps to line up the club face squarely. I believe that the most successful way to putt is with firm, passive wrists, especially through the impact zone, and one of the best ways to ensure this is to adopt the reverse overlap grip. This is where the left forefinger is taken off the grip, and allowed to overlap the fingers of the right hand. The normal overlap and interlocking grips that most people use for hitting other shots fail to give the additional firmness at the back of the left wrist that the reverse overlap grip provides. So to adopt the correct grip you should do the following:

1 Stand with the putter face square to the target, palms either side of the grip and parallel to the club face, with the thumbs at the front of the grip (Fig 2.1a).
2 Grip the putter with both hands completely on the grip, i.e. ten fingers, then remove the left forefinger from the grip (Fig 2.1b).
3 Slide the right hand up to butt against the left, then place the left forefinger over the fingers of the right hand (Fig 2.1c).

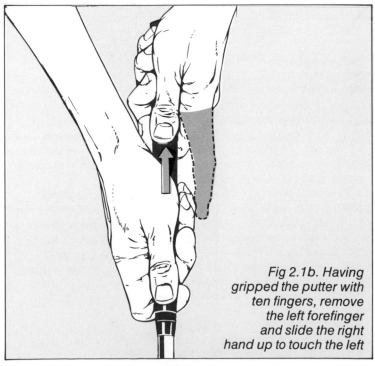

Fig 2.1b. Having gripped the putter with ten fingers, remove the left forefinger and slide the right hand up to touch the left

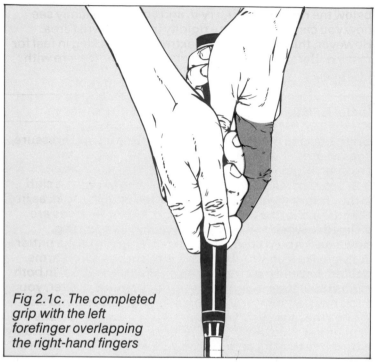

Fig 2.1c. The completed
grip with the left
forefinger overlapping
the right-hand fingers

You should find that the grip of the putter passes more
through the middle of the left palm, than it does when
gripping other clubs. This is because you stand further over
the ball than for any other shot, and therefore grip the club in
a more upright manner. I have changed many golfers' grips
to the reverse overlap, which may feel strange initially, but
like any other aspect of golf, if you practise it, even for five or
ten minutes before you go out to play, it will soon become
comfortable and automatic.

This is the putting grip that I and many hundreds of
professional golfers use, and it helps to ensure that the back
of the left wrist does not collapse inwards through the
stroke. Some professionals use adaptations of this grip –
you may have seen Seve Ballesteros placing his right
forefinger slightly down the shaft, whereas Nancy Lopez
places hers completely down the right side. This has the
effect of firming up the right wrist, and you may find it
helpful.

In order to create even more firmness and control in the
left hand and wrist, some golfers, perhaps most notably
Bernhard Langer, place their hands on the grip, with the left

below the right (Fig 2.2). Try it, and you will instantly see how you can sustain more rigidity in the left wrist area. However, this may seem too extreme and lacking in feel for many golfers, so I would suggest that you persevere with the reverse overlap.

Grip pressure

One hears and reads many different ideas on grip pressure, and it is probably a personal preference as much as anything. However, since we are trying to eliminate unwanted independent hand action, I like to grip the club firmly, rather than lightly. I work on the principle that, as in the golf swing, the tighter we grip, the less the hands are inclined to work, and apply that theory to my putting. However, I would add a proviso that I do not grip the putter in a vice-like fashion which tenses my hands or forearms. Instead, I would describe my grip as firm, and equal in both hands rather than light, and it works for me. However, you should experiment with different grip pressures, and find the one that suits you best. Certainly, on very long putts your grip should be firmer, since you are using considerably more force than for a three foot putt, and you must ensure that you have total control of the putter head.

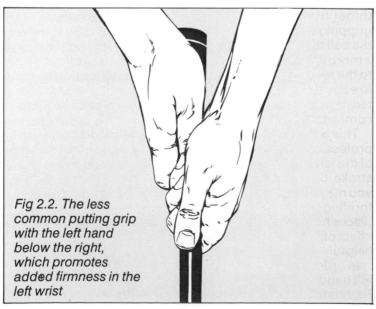

Fig 2.2. The less common putting grip with the left hand below the right, which promotes added firmness in the left wrist

CHAPTER 3

The address position

Like all shots in golf, how you stand to the ball will affect how the club is swung. In putting, you stand closer to the ball than for any other shot, and this gives you the opportunity to swing the clubhead on a straighter line than for other shots. However, it is important to understand that the clubhead moves away from the ball in a straight line, and the further back it travels, the more inside the ball to target line it moves. It is only on the shortest of putts that it will move in a straight line.

Posture

In the long game, you bend from the hips in order to create

Fig 3.1. The good points to note in this address position are that the player has bent forward from the hips, which places the eyes directly above the ball to target line. The putter is squarely aimed over an intermediate target and the wrists are held high for added firmness. The shoulders and forearms are parallel to the target line

space in which your arms can swing – you must do likewise in putting. The extent to which you bend over will vary from player to player depending on your build, but make sure you bend sufficiently to allow your arms to hang freely from the shoulder joints. Some of the best putters in the world have adopted a very low position over the ball, whereas others choose to stand more upright. So you can experiment as to which feels more suitable. If you choose to stand fairly upright, your arms will be almost straight when you putt, much like Ben Crenshaw; but should you crouch lower over the ball, you will have to bend your arms at the elbow, or grip further down the putter.

However, another important aspect to consider in bending forward, is where your eyes are in relation to the ball to target line. In putting, you have the best chance of setting your eyes directly over the line the ball will travel, which must help with the direction (Fig 3.1). So, having taken your address position, you can easily check this by dropping a ball from under your left eye, and seeing where it

Fig 3.2. The left shoulder is higher than the right, the hands are just ahead of the ball, which is forward in the stance inside the left heel. The elbows are fairly close to the side, not sticking out

hits the ground. Ideally it should either hit the ball you are putting, or drop just inside it. If it is way outside or inside, you need to adjust either the ball position or your posture until you meet the necessary requirement.

Lining up

As with my long shots, I find it useful to have an intermediate target, about two feet ahead of the ball, over which I want to set the ball rolling. I therefore line up the putter square to that spot.

I would always recommend that you try to set your shoulders and forearms parallel to the ball to target line, since this will make it much easier to swing the clubhead in the correct direction. Also ensure that your left shoulder is higher than the right (Fig 3.2). This should happen naturally, since the right hand is lower than the left on the grip, but it is easy to allow the left shoulder to drop, and the right to come forward. This action also tends to kink the back of the left hand too much – just what you want to avoid!

How you place your feet and hips is a more personal choice. I tend to have mine open, i.e. a line drawn across my

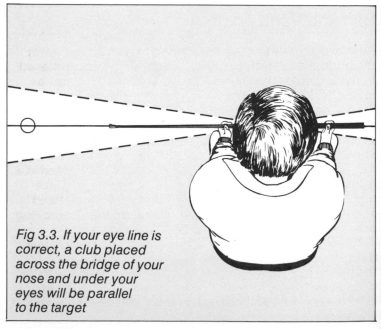

Fig 3.3. If your eye line is correct, a club placed across the bridge of your nose and under your eyes will be parallel to the target

14

feet and hips would point left of parallel, since I find this gives me a clearer path for my arms and club on the through swing. The width of stance is dependent on your build, and is also a matter of preference, but do not be too extreme. Few top-class golfers putt with their feet either together or very wide apart.

It is also vital that your eyes are parallel to the target line, and you can check this by taking your address position. Now without moving your head, in both hands hold the shaft of the putter across the bridge of your nose, and under your eyes (Fig 3.3). If the shaft is not parallel to your target, then neither are your eyes.

Weight distribution

In putting, you should try to hit the ball at the bottom of the putter's arc, or just on the way up. Therefore I feel that your weight should be evenly distributed. It will be more towards the balls of your feet than the heels, and for added stability some people like to have more weight on the inside of each foot. It is essential that you feel balanced, since the head must remain still throughout the putting stroke.

Ball and hand position

As I have already said, you are trying to contact the ball at the bottom or slightly on the upswing, so it must be placed fairly forward in the stance near the left foot. This may be inside the heel for some golfers, or opposite the left toe for others, depending on your stance. I also like the putter shaft to be sloping slightly towards the target, rather than vertical, since this means that at the start my hands are just ahead of the club face, which will help them to stay that way throughout the putt (Fig 3.2). This point can be checked in a mirror. I hold my wrists quite high rather than low, since high or arched wrists will help eliminate unwanted hand action, and make the swing path straighter, thus improving accuracy.

The address position for putting is a more personal one than for any other shot. If you putt well, and yet do none of the things that I believe are important, far be it for me to change a winning formula. But when I teach someone to putt, the grip and address position detailed in the last two chapters are the fundamental points I instil in a pupil.

CHAPTER 4

How to strike putts consistently

To putt well the clubhead must be swung on a very shallow arc, so that there is no suggestion of hitting down on the ball. Instead, it is *rolled* forwards as the putter approaches from very close to the ground. On short putts the putter will swing back and through on almost a straight line, whereas on longer putts, the clubhead must start to move inside on the backswing, strike the ball while it is moving directly towards the target and will then tend to swing back to the inside (Fig 4.1).

To guarantee a shallow arc, keep the clubhead close to the ground by moving the arms and hands away together. Any

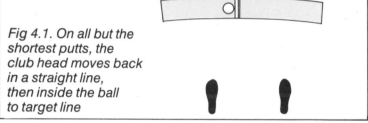

Fig 4.1. On all but the shortest putts, the club head moves back in a straight line, then inside the ball to target line

Fig 4.2 a, b and c. In a good putting action the angle at the back of the hands and arms remains the same throughout the stroke, keeping the club head low to the ground. In Fig 4.2c. you will see that the whole of the putter grip has been kept moving towards the target after impact

a

hint of the hands moving and the arms staying still, will see the clubhead leave the ground quite sharply, and you will tend to hit down too much on the putt. Instead, the whole action should feel firm. In fact, I like to use my forearms, rather than my hands, to swing the putter, thus keeping my hands out of the action on all but the very longest of putts. Some people like to feel that the left hand and arm push the clubhead back, while the right hand and arm swing the putter forward, and I have to admit that there have been times when this method has worked for me. You may like to work on keeping the whole of the grip on the putter, or the back of the left hand moving towards the hole, both of which again promote the very action required. The method you select is a personal choice, and one that may change from day to day or from week to week, but those golfers whose hands work independently, will need to concentrate on their forearms moving.

Throughout the stroke you should try to preserve the angle set between the hands and forearms at address since, if you can do this, the unit of your hands and arms will be moving together (Fig 4.2 a, b and c). It is a good idea to check the swing path of the putter by laying a club on the ground just outside the putter head. In the backswing the clubhead should not touch the shaft, and should move inside on the longer putts. The whole stroke must be made smoothly and in an unhurried manner, much like a pendulum. As you

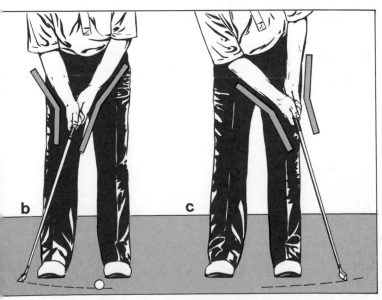

complete each putt, check that the back of your left hand has not collapsed inwards but has retained the original angle. You should start with short straight putts of about three feet, making certain that the club face is square to the target, then try to hit each one from the middle of the putter to the middle of the hole. You should feel that the putter head moves directly towards the hole after the ball has been struck, since this gives a better chance of hitting the ball down the desired track.

Incidentally, most putters these days have a mark to indicate the middle of the putter, but you can check this is in the correct spot, by holding the club between your thumb and forefinger and letting the shaft hang vertically. Take a coin and tap along the face until you hit the spot where the putter swings straight back without the toe or heel twisting (Fig 4.3). This is the middle, or sweet spot as it is known, and you should always address the ball lined up with this spot.

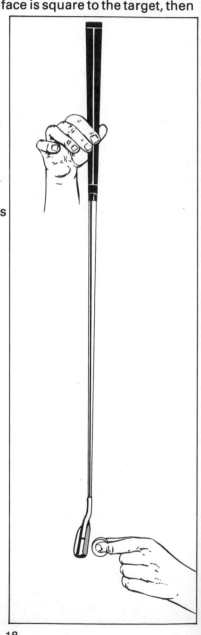

Fig 4.3. You can find the sweet spot of your putter by using a coin to tap the face. When it swings straight back without the heel or toe twisting, you have found the spot, which you should mark

Judging distance

You must accelerate through a putt, so it is essential to have the correct length of backswing; one that is too long encourages you to decelerate into the ball, whereas one that is too short will make you use your hands to flick at it at the last minute. It is also important that you learn to strike the ball from the middle of the putter if you are to become adept at judging distance. For example, you are on the first green with a fifteen foot putt; you hit it out of the heel and it pulls up well short of the hole. On the second green you have a similar length putt. Having been short on the first green you hit it a bit harder, but this time you strike it out of the middle of the putter and it goes six feet past. So you go to the third green knowing no more about the pace of the greens than when you started, and are thoroughly confused.

Therefore, it is important to work on a good strike in developing your putting, rather than becoming too concerned initially about holing the putts. In fact, you might strike the putt well but read it wrong – this tends to improve with experience. When I have a long putt, I always try to view it from the side, since this gives a better sense of the true distance. I stand with the ball on my right, halfway along the line and try to imagine the pace at which the ball will leave the putter in order to finish in or near the hole. I stand beside the ball and have a couple of practice putts looking at the hole, and imagining the ball rolling along the line into it. I then use the same strength putt to hit the ball. You may think that this routine is rather time consuming, but you can look at the putt while others are putting, or whilst you are walking onto the green – it need not take too long.

Obviously, the longer you play, the easier it becomes to compute quickly how the pace and slope of the green, together with the length of the putt, determine how hard you should hit the ball, but this can only be calculated if you strike the ball well. In fact, I tell my pupils that if they wish to test how purely they strike a putt, they should hit long putts, where such imperfections are highlighted. On a three foot putt, you may well get away with a putt not hit right out of the middle, since it has not far to travel, but a 30 footer out of the heel or toe will pull up well short of the target.

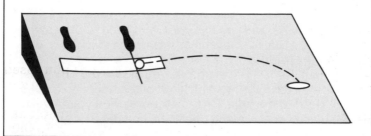

Fig 4.4a. On a putt breaking from left to right, play the ball further forward in the stance than normal to guard against pushing the putt

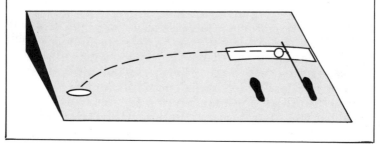

Fig 4.4b. On a putt breaking from right to left, play the ball further back in the stance than normal to guard against pulling the putt

Head still

It is essential that on all putts you keep your head and, for that matter, your whole frame as still as possible. Any movement of the head or swaying of the body before the ball is struck will only be detrimental to the result. So having addressed the ball, try to allow your hands and arms only to swing the putter. You will find that your shoulders will move as well in response to your arms, but you should not try to move them consciously as this can lead to swaying off the ball. Look at the back of the ball until it is struck, and then keep your head still and eyes focused on the spot where the ball was placed until it is well on its way. Some golfers favour listening for the ball to drop in the hole, which is a good idea. I like to ask people to keep the head and eyes still and guess where the ball has gone. They may not always guess correctly, but it does have the desired effect of stopping them looking up too soon.

How to practise your putting

As I have said, you should practise striking the putt well, perhaps giving yourself marks out of ten for each putt based on the quality of strike and direction, rather than getting too concerned about always holing out. Few greens are absolutely smooth, and even machines set up to hole putts in laboratory conditions do not succeed every time. So your practice should be to set up correctly, with the club face square to the target, and to make a smooth putt along the correct swing path. Use a club laid down just outside the putter head and parallel to the target to help or, if you practise indoors, you can use the skirting board to check the line of your swing. Remember that it should be straight back on only the shortest of putts, and then the putter head must swing to the inside.

Some time should be spent practising one-handed, using each hand in turn – you will then appreciate better how each hand works through the stroke. Practise also with the left hand below the right, and then switch back to your usual grip. This highlights how the left hand should feel throughout the stroke, and promotes the necessary firmness. Putting with your eyes shut will increase your sense of feel, and focus your attention on your action. To develop a positive action and attitude, practise a straight, slightly uphill putt, from about three to four feet. This needs to be struck authoritatively, which is a good asset in putting. However, you must not neglect putts from any angle, so after the uphill putts, you should practise the same putt downhill and then across the slope. On right to left putts, you will find it useful to play the ball a little nearer the middle of the stance, as this helps to ensure that you do not pull the putt, while with a left to right borrow, play the ball more forward to guard against pushing it (Fig. 4.4).

It always helps to compete against someone on the putting green, so do this as often as possible; failing that, putt just one ball and count your score.

CHAPTER 5

How to read greens

Having played in hundreds of Pro-Ams, I know that all club golfers could improve their putting statistics if they could read the greens better. I try to read most of my partner's putts, providing they wish me to do so, as a result of which they then seem to putt with greater confidence, and in the right direction. Much of the information needed to read a putt can be gleaned before you are on the green just by observing the lie of the surrounding land. So as you walk towards the green, if the land on the right is higher than that on the left, the chances are that the whole of the putting green will slope in that direction. The same applies if you are walking up a slope towards the green: it is likely that the green will slope upwards from front to back. It does not take a genius to work out these facts — you just need to be observant. However, these generalities do not apply every time, and you must always check the line of your putt.

Developing a routine

Over the years I have developed a routine: I walk to a spot behind the cup and look back to my ball trying to judge the line. I found that I could always estimate my partner's line reasonably accurately while I attended the pin and thus I started to read my putts from the same position. You may wish only to look from behind the ball, and if that works for you, then stay with that method. While I walk back to my ball I view the putt from the side, also checking that there are no stones or pitch marks on my line. Then I have a quick glance from behind the ball to confirm my first observations on the line, and I also select an intermediate target about two or three feet ahead on the line of the putt over which I can aim. It is not always possible to find something identifiable on the line, but if I can do so, it helps me enormously to line up correctly. I personally can learn a lot by walking between my ball and the hole, since I can often feel through my feet any slope that may be there. This all takes time, and when playing professionally we take longer than the average club golfer to get round, so far be it from me to encourage slow play!

However, do try to adopt a routine that you repeat for

each putt, bar the very short ones, and one that does *not* take too much time. It is always a good idea to watch your playing partner's putts. I like to imagine that I have his putt and try to judge how hard I would have hit it, check that against my partner's stroke, and then watch how the putt breaks. From this I can learn something about the pace and borrow on the green. So again, it is a matter of being observant rather than clever!

How pace affects borrow

The pace of the green, apart from any slopes, is affected by the length of the grass and whether it is wet or dry. Obviously, a wet green with long grass is going to be slower than one that has just been cut and is dry, so allow for these variables.

Having read the line, have a couple of practice putts to judge how hard to hit the ball. I tend to see the ball dying into the hole, or at most going a foot past, in which case I have to allow the maximum borrow for any putt. If you like to putt more aggressively, then the line will be straighter, but bear in mind that if you miss the hole, the putt may be longer than you would have liked (Fig 5.1). It is fine to be aggressive on

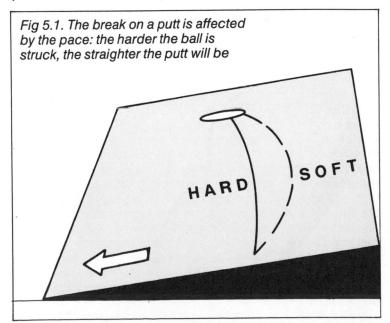

Fig 5.1. The break on a putt is affected by the pace: the harder the ball is struck, the straighter the putt will be

HARD   SOFT

uphill putts, but be careful with the downhill ones when it is probably better to trickle them allowing for plenty of break. Remember that uphill putts never break as much as downhill (Fig 5.2). If your putt has more than one break, it is the one nearest the hole that will be most influential on your choice of line. The early breaks will not affect the ball so much since it will be rolling more quickly than when it is near the hole. If you are unlucky enough to have a putt, say of ten feet, with two different breaks, then you will have to make allowances for the ball to break in two different directions (Fig 5.3). Sometimes one break can offset the other, and the line becomes almost straight, but I think that your perception of the situation would be improved on this occasion by looking at the putt from more than one direction.

Two-tier greens

Two-tier greens can also be tricky, not only from the reading point of view, but also in determining the pace. Not all courses have distinct two-tier greens, and thus many golfers are not accustomed to putting on them, and their

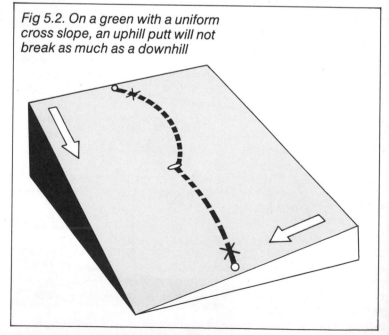

Fig 5.2. On a green with a uniform cross slope, an uphill putt will not break as much as a downhill

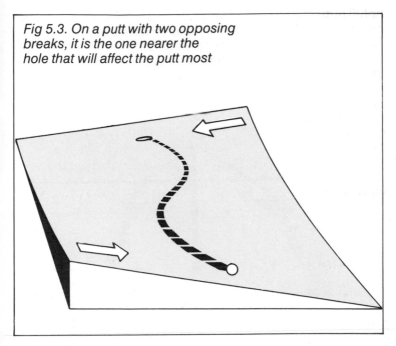

Fig 5.3. On a putt with two opposing breaks, it is the one nearer the hole that will affect the putt most

judgement of line and length is affected greatly. You must decide first to what extent the slope will make the ball break, and then choose the pace. If you are putting across the slope, rather than straight up it, remember that the ball will curve towards the lower level as it climbs (Fig 5.4). It may be affected also by any other slopes on the top tier, so you can understand why these are difficult putts. If you have to putt down a two-tier slope, depending on the position of the pin and the pace of the green, you may find that you have only to putt the ball to the edge of the top tier and the slope will do the rest. But remember that when a ball is moving slowly, it takes more borrow.

Grain or nap on the green

In some parts of the world, the grain or nap on the green can affect the putt greatly; so much so that sometimes a ball can appear to be breaking up a hill. You can see which way the grass grows by the change in shading. If the grain is lying with the putt, which means it will roll faster, then the grass will appear light and shiny. However, if it lies against the putt, thus slowing the pace, it looks darker and dull. A putt

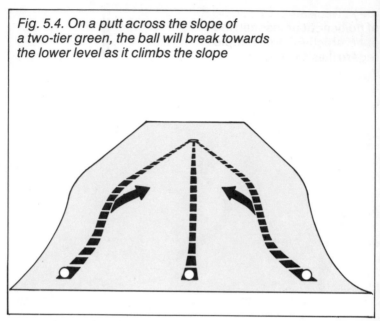

Fig. 5.4. On a putt across the slope of a two-tier green, the ball will break towards the lower level as it climbs the slope

across the grain will tend to move in whichever direction the grain is growing, so that if the grain lies in the opposite direction to the slope, there will be a tendency to straighten the line. In Great Britain there are few courses that have grainy greens, but in parts of Europe, the United States and other hotter climates, there are many courses where the grain must be considered when reading a putt.

Plumb bobbing

This is a method of reading the green, whereby standing behind the ball you hold the putter between finger and thumb so that it hangs vertically (Fig. 5.5). Looking down the line, with your master eye only open, cover the ball with the lower shaft of the putter and then see which side of the hole the grip end is positioned. This will indicate the higher side of the hole and the direction in which the green slopes. It does not necessarily give you the exact amount of borrow to allow, but the further away from the hole the grip appears, the more slope on the green. However, this method works only if you are standing on ground that slopes in the same direction as that near the hole, and you are perpendicular to that ground. So plumb bobbing can be used successfully only on certain putts, and is of no benefit unless carried out correctly. Some people regard it as a useful system, whereas others never understand it. However, you should try everything, and if it works you keep it: otherwise reject it.

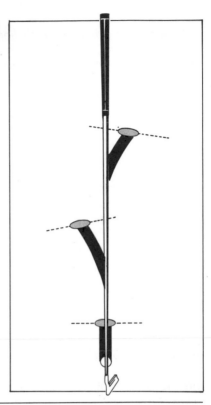

Fig 5.5. With the plumb-bob method, stand behind the ball and hold the club so that it hangs vertically. With the lower end of the shaft covering the ball, note where the grip end is in relation to the hole and this will indicate in which direction the ground slopes

Visualization

You really must develop a great sense of imagination in putting, especially for those more difficult putts. In order to do this, you must be able to visualize how the ball will roll. Many players like to imagine that there is a three foot wide circle around the hole, and that they are putting into that area. If you feel that helps you, then use it, but I always prefer to imagine the ball going into the hole. On long difficult putts I know that it is unlikely that I will hole them, but it gives me a more definite target. With middle range putts I try to get a strong mental picture of the ball going into the hole when I take my couple of practice putts. I visualize the exact line the ball must take, and sense the pace at which it must be moving. You too can develop this ability, which is essential if you are to become a first-class putter. So put a little more thought into your putting, both on the practice green and on the course, and I am sure that you will be pleasantly surprised at the improvement.

27

CHAPTER 6

Which putter?

Nowadays there is such a variety of putters available that it is difficult to know which to choose. However, I can give you a few guidelines which would be worth considering regardless of the type of putter you select.

1 The length

Obviously those golfers who are tall, or stand very upright to putt, need a longer putter than a short person or someone who bends over a long way. Find one that does not leave too many inches sticking out from your left hand, since this may catch on your thighs through the stroke.

2 The grip

I would strongly recommend a putter grip that is flat at the front, as this will not only help you to grip the club correctly, but also to line up the face. However, do make sure that the grip has been put on squarely, which, unfortunately, is not always the case.

3 The lie

The lie refers to the angle at which the shaft leaves the putter head, and ideally the bottom of the putter should be flat on the ground at address. However, there are some superb putters, notably Seve Ballesteros, who address the ball with the toe of the putter in the air, but you should aim to find a putter with the correct lie. I would recommend a fairly upright putter, since it will help you to putt on a straighter swing path than a flat one (Fig 6.1). However, personal preference, and what you feel most comfortable and confident with, will have to play a part in your choice.

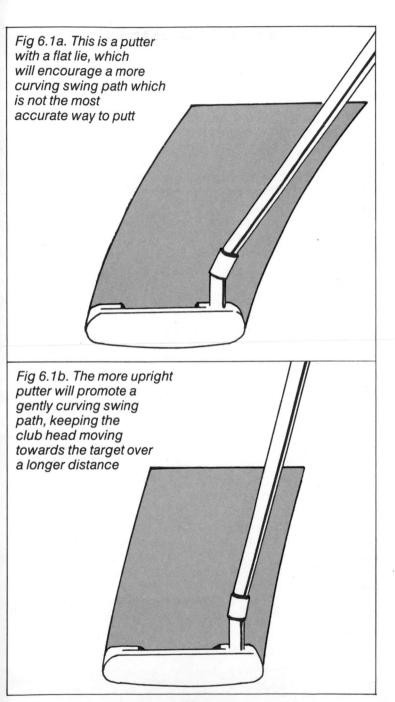

Fig 6.1a. This is a putter with a flat lie, which will encourage a more curving swing path which is not the most accurate way to putt

Fig 6.1b. The more upright putter will promote a gently curving swing path, keeping the club head moving towards the target over a longer distance

4 The weight

There are many different weights of putter, and again it
really is a matter for personal preference. Heavy putters are
harder for you to twitch off-line, their weight making a
pendulum action slightly easier, but you may find that you
get more feel from a light putter. Some professionals like to
vary the weight according to the pace of the greens, but
keeping the same model putter. Experiment with a variety
of weights, perhaps even putting some lead tape on the
back of yours to increase the weight.

5 Style of putter

There are many different styles, such as mallet-headed,
centre-shafted, blade, or Ping type, and again it is a matter
of what you like best (Fig 6.2.). However, it is a scientific fact
that the Ping or a Ping-type putter, which has more weight at
the heel and toe, creates a bigger sweet spot, and therefore
a larger area of strike. Probably more top professionals
currently use this type than any other putter, so it must have
some special qualities.

Consider all these aspects before you buy your next putter,
and try a few out in the professional's shop, or borrow a
friend's before you make a final decision. If you find the right
one, you will probably never part with it.

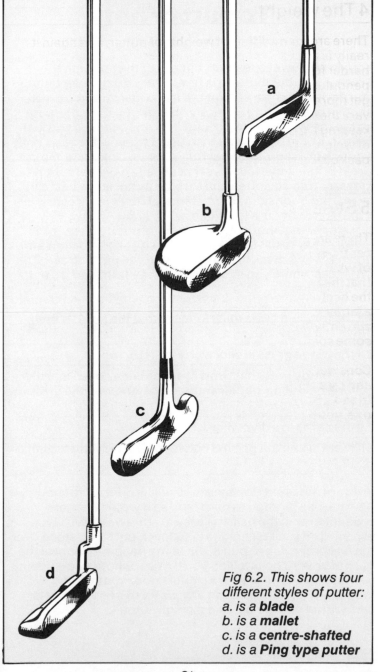

Fig 6.2. This shows four different styles of putter:
*a. is a **blade***
*b. is a **mallet***
*c. is a **centre-shafted***
*d. is a **Ping type putter***

CHAPTER 7

To putt or not

You do not have to restrict your use of the putter to the green alone, but there are a few factors to consider before you decide where else to use it. If you just miss the green, and the ball is sitting up nicely on a short cut fringe, there is no reason why you cannot putt it. In this instance you just have to hit the ball harder than usual to allow for its journey through the slightly longer fringe grass. Links courses in Great Britain have fairways that usually have very short grass, and so you often find that the putter is the best club even from a considerable distance off the green, especially if the alternative is a formidable chip shot. Always remember that more often than not, a poorly hit putt will give a better result than a poorly hit chip, so if you miss the green always check first whether you can putt the ball. The instances where you should steer away from using a putter are as follows:

1 If the fringe grass is quite long, so that the ball is sitting down in it (Fig 7.1a).

2 If the fringe grass is very wet (Fig 7.1b).

3 If the fringe grass has grown, or has been cut so that the ball will be rolling significantly against the way the grass lies (Fig 7.1c).

4 If the ball is in a divot (Fig 7.1d).

5 If there is uneven ground between your ball and the hole (Fig 7.1e).

In any of these circumstances, it will be difficult to know just how the ball is going to react, and so it would be more prudent to chip the ball. It is easy to shy away from chipping, especially if your technique is suspect, but if you stand over the ball preparing to putt it, but some nagging doubt at the back of your mind is telling you that you should be chipping, the indecision can lead to a lack of concentration and, inevitably, a poor result. So always try to be 100 per cent certain that you are playing the right shot.

Fig 7.1. If you miss the green, do not putt the ball if:

a. sitting down in rather long grass

b. the fringe grass is very wet

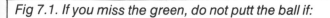

c. the grain of the grass is lying against the ball

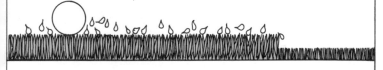

d. the ball is in a divot

e. the ground between the ball and the green is uneven

CHAPTER 8

The art of chipping

Chipping is essentially a very simple part of golf, and one that can save you many shots. If you could guarantee getting down in two nearly every time you just missed the green, your handicap would drop considerably, so do not neglect this department. The main point to remember is that you are trying to hit slightly down on the ball, which will loft it in the air sufficiently to land *just* on the green and roll up to the pin (Fig 8.1).

The set up

Because chipping involves very little movement or leg action, you set up with your feet close together, and feet and hips slightly open to the target. This allows the arms to swing through the ball unimpeded and gives you a better aspect of the shot. However, I would recommend that you keep your shoulders parallel to the ball to target line, since

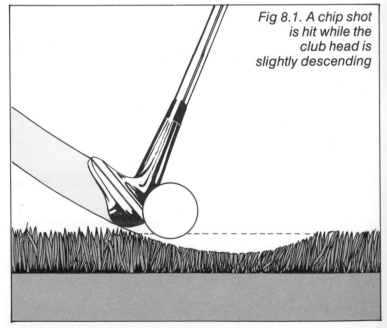

Fig 8.1. A chip shot is hit while the club head is slightly descending

this will ensure that the club is swung in the correct direction. You must bend forwards from the hips, so that your arms have room in which to swing, and this will bring your weight forwards onto the balls of your feet. About sixty to seventy per cent of your weight is placed on the left foot, and the ball is positioned well back in the stance, so that it is quite close to the right foot (Fig 8.2). Many players make the

Fig 8.2. At address, the weight and hands should be forward and the ball back. The forearms and shaft form a 'Y' shape

mistake of playing the ball too far forward in the stance, so check the ball position by taking your set up, then place a club behind the ball and just withdraw your right foot backwards. This will enable you to see where the ball is in relation to your left foot – it should be inside the left heel. The exact amount will depend on the lie, which I will explain later, but it is better to err by having the ball too far back since this will encourage the slightly descending strike that you require.

It is also essential that your hands are well ahead of the ball at address so that your left arm and the shaft form at least a straight line. You can best check this and the ball position by looking in the mirror. This address position does tend to de-loft the club a little so that a 7 iron will become more like a 6 iron. One of the best ways I have found to help my pupils adopt the correct address position is to remember it as two forward and one back. The two forward

Fig 8.3a. The backswing is made by swinging the 'Y' shape of the forearms and shaft

are: the weight and the hands; and the one back is: the ball position. It is advisable to grip down on the club, since this gives you additional control and feel. Most people use their normal golf grip for chipping, but if you putt using the reverse overlap grip (as I hope you do after reading the first part of this book) you might like to experiment with that grip, since it does give extra firmness in the left hand – an important feature of a good chipping action.

The stroke

As you address the ball, your forearms form a letter 'Y', and you should chip the ball, simply by swinging the 'Y' shape (Fig 8.3a). In this way, your hands will play only a small role in the shot, while the forearms are the major contributors. Ideally the left hand and arm swing the club back and

Fig 8.3b. At impact the 'Y' is still intact so that the hands are ahead of the ball and the back of the left wrist is still firm. The right knee eases towards the target

Fig 8.4. If the left hand does not keep moving towards the target, it collapses and the ball is hit off the wrong part of the club

through the ball, with the most important point being that at impact the hands are ahead of the ball (Fig 8.3b) and the left arm continues moving through the shot. If it stops, the right hand carries on, the back of the left wrist collapses (Fig 8.4) and the bottom edge of the club usually hits the ball, resulting in a very poor shot, which more often than not shoots across the green and off the other side. The address position advocated will encourage the club to be swung back on a gently ascending arc, thus permitting the slightly descending strike that you need. Any attempt to help the ball in the air by trying to scoop it will defeat the whole object, so hit down slightly on the ball and allow the loft of the club to do the work. To improve the contact, you will find it helpful to keep the whole of the grip moving towards the target (Fig 8.5). When the left hand stops, usually in an effort to scoop the ball in the air with the right hand, the end of the grip stops too, but by keeping the whole of the grip moving towards the target, the back of the left hand remains firm.

I like to feel that my left hand and, more importantly, my left forearm swing the club, but if you can obtain a better feel for the shot by using your right hand and arm, then so be it. But remember that the angle at the back of the right hand must remain constant, especially through impact. On longer chip shots the wrists do give a little on the backswing, but the same firm left wrist position at impact is essential. The length of the swing will obviously depend on which club you use and the length of the shot, but you should always take a couple of practice swings, visualizing where the shot should land. Do not make the backswing too long so that you decelerate at impact, but neither should you make it too short, or the hands will tend to flick at the ball at the last minute, causing a mis-hit. Make sure that you accelerate smoothly, and try to make the backswing and throughswing the same length. There is virtually no weight transference on the backswing, but you will find it helpful to ease the right knee towards the target as the ball is struck. This will prevent the hands from closing the club face, and also keep the swing on line. Keep your head still and eyes down until well after the ball is struck – any temptation to look up too quickly will affect the quality of strike. The stroke itself should be smooth and unhurried; it is accuracy, not power, that is essential.

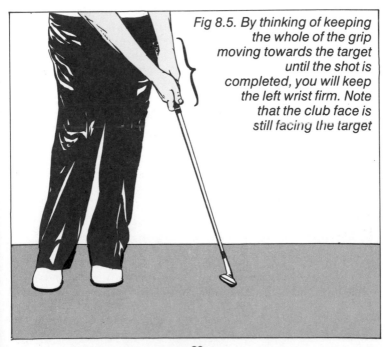

Fig 8.5. By thinking of keeping the whole of the grip moving towards the target until the shot is completed, you will keep the left wrist firm. Note that the club face is still facing the target

Which club for which shot?

When deciding on the club for a chip shot, you should select one that will land the ball on the edge of the green and then run up to the hole. It is therefore useful to know how the ball will react with different clubs, i.e. what proportion of its journey the ball will spend in the air and on the ground. It is not essential to know initially how each club reacts, but by understanding the flight characteristics of a few clubs, you can work from there. So the following should be treated as a suitable guideline:

Fig 8.6. This shows the proportion of air to ground time with different clubs

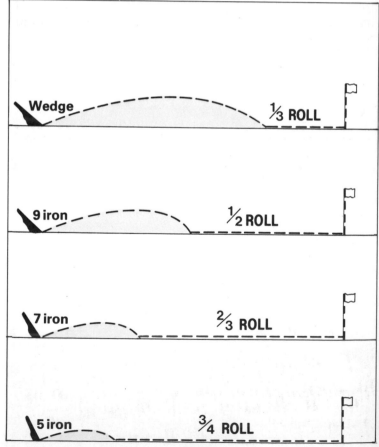

Wedge ⅓ ROLL

9 iron ½ ROLL

7 iron ⅔ ROLL

5 iron ¾ ROLL

Wedge – two-thirds in the air, one-third on the ground.

9 iron – half the time in the air, half on the ground.

7 iron – one-third in the air, two-thirds on the ground.

5 iron – a quarter in the air, three-quarters on the ground.

All shown in Fig 8.6

By remembering how these four clubs work, you will be prepared for most situations, and experience will enable you to appreciate how all the clubs work and which you prefer using. Obviously when using those with more loft, i.e. the higher numbered clubs, the ball spends more time in the air than on the ground, whereas with the straight faced clubs, like a 3 or 4 iron, the ball spends less time in the air than on the ground. However, choice of club is often a personal preference, and some professionals may use one club, usually a wedge or sand wedge, for all their chipping and pitching, but they have plenty of experience in adapting how the club face sits and where to position the ball to vary the height and roll of the shot. You should try to keep to the principle of using the most appropriate club for the shot.

One way to appreciate how different clubs affect the ball's height and roll, is to hit shots with various clubs from one spot onto a green, but using the same strength swing. You will see how the ball travels varying distances – the shots with the low numbered clubs going the furthest. Choice of club is related to how hard you hit the shot, and so there are many combinations that can be used. Practise with the clubs I have suggested and get a working knowledge of them. You can then expand on this groundwork, but always try to land the ball just on the green and let it roll up to the pin.

Bad lies

If the ball is lying in a divot, or well down in the grass, you must make sure that it is well back in the stance, even opposite the right toe, and that the hands and weight are well ahead of the ball. Swing the clubhead back on a slightly steeper path than usual, allowing the right wrist to cock a little, and be certain to hit down on the ball. The throughswing may be curtailed somewhat, and the ball will come out low and run. If you have only a short distance to cover, it may be best to use a sand iron for this shot, as its extra loft will offset the loft lost by this particular address position.

CHAPTER 9

The long chip and run

When the ball lands only a few yards off the green, it is usual to play a chip and run shot, or putt the ball. It is only when a ball is perhaps fifteen or twenty yards off the putting surface that you may be torn between a chip and run, or a pitch shot.

A pitch is an elevated shot that applies backspin to the ball, preventing it from running too much on landing. It is the more difficult of the two shots to play, requiring additional hand action, which, if not timed correctly, can create the more destructive shot. So often club golfers feel that at any time they are off the green they should be pitching the ball, but instead you can extend the action of the chip shot, simply by making a longer backswing and

Fig 9.1. As the arms are swung back, there is no conscious effort to cock the wrists but they will naturally break a little in response to the weight of the club head

increasing the leg action. You should adopt a similar set up but use a slightly wider stance; position the ball about three to four inches inside the left heel and grip nearer the end of the club. The choice of club is dictated by the situation, but generally you will be using the higher numbered clubs, since you still want the ball to land on the green. As your arms swing the clubhead away, with the left arm in command, do not make any conscious effort to use your hands. Your wrists will naturally cock in response the weight of the club head (Fig 9.1). Your weight will transfer a little onto your right leg and then, as your arms swing down and through, your weight must move back to the left side. It is not a steep angle of attack on the ball, more of a 'U' shaped swing, and providing you do not grip too tightly, the little amount of wrist break developed in the backswing will naturally unwind at impact. The left arm should be dominant throughout, and the left wrist must stay firm, and

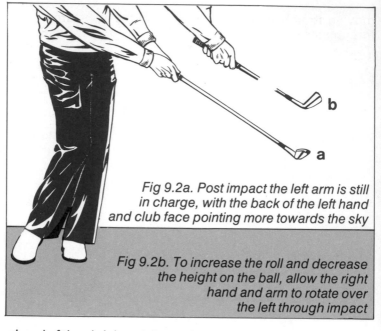

Fig 9.2a. Post impact the left arm is still in charge, with the back of the left hand and club face pointing more towards the sky

Fig 9.2b. To increase the roll and decrease the height on the ball, allow the right hand and arm to rotate over the left through impact

ahead of the club head through impact.

For normal shots the right hand and arm should not cross over the left, so that the club face points more towards the sky at the completion of the shot, (Fig 9.2a). However, if you are playing into a strong headwind, or the pin is at the back of a very long green, allowing the right hand and arm to cross a little over the left (Fig 9.2b), will have the effect of de-lofting the club, and making the ball fly lower and run more on landing.

The swing path

Since the club head is now being swung back further than for the short chip shot from the fringe, you must allow it to swing to the inside, so that it returns from the inside and strikes the ball while moving directly towards the target. I like to teach people using the clock face as an analogy. Imagine that the ball is in the middle of a clock face and you are standing at 6 o'clock, with your shoulders parallel to the ball to target line; 3 o'clock is on the right and 9 o'clock is on the left (Fig 9.3). Initially the club head swings straight back and then, as the body starts to turn, it is swung inwards and upwards between 3 and 4 o'clock. Ideally it is swung back down on the same path, the ball is struck while the club is moving straight towards 9 and then, as the body turns through the shot, the club moves back inside towards 8 o'clock.

So having progressed far enough off the green to demand a fuller swing, you must let the club head swing inside a little on the backswing as the body turns. Admittedly, with the shorter irons the club head will not swing as much to the inside as for the longer clubs, but by having it in mind that you are trying to swing from between 3 and 4 o'clock to 9 o'clock, it will help you to improve the direction of your shots.

If the ball is sitting badly, i.e. in a divot or in short rough, you will need to position it further back in the stance and swing the club back more steeply, creating more of a 'V' shaped swing.

Too many club golfers try to play a high pitch shot whenever they miss the green. Instead, you should think about playing the long chip and run, as it is the safer percentage shot, and one that is easy to execute. But like any shot in golf, you will have to practise and experiment a little to appreciate just how the ball will react.

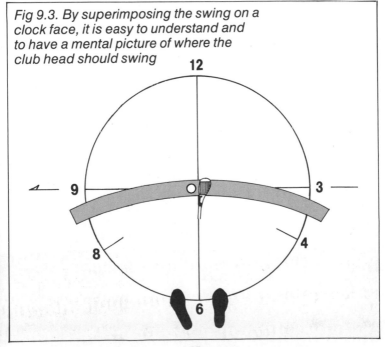

Fig 9.3. By superimposing the swing on a clock face, it is easy to understand and to have a mental picture of where the club head should swing

CHAPTER 10

The short pitch

When you have to get maximum height and minimum roll on a shot, then you should use a pitch shot. In this chapter I will deal with the short pitch that you will have to play from just around the green, maybe over a bunker. It has to be admitted that this is not one of the easiest shots in golf, requiring as it does, well-timed hand action, a reasonable lie and confidence.

Many players are so afraid of this shot that they rush to complete it and lack any sense of discipline in how they should approach it, so try not to quicken your actions.

Fig 10.1a. Set up with a narrow, open stance, with the weight favouring the left leg. The hands are just ahead of the ball which is inside the left heel. The left arm and shaft form a straight line

However, since this is one of those shots that, if not executed correctly, can ruin your score, I feel that the beginner, the higher handicap player, and any golfers who are not totally confident, might do better by using a wedge or sand wedge and employing an action similar to that used in the rather more passive handed long chip and run shot. This is not admitting defeat, but rather a matter of being sensible and realistic about your ability; it is also the shot that, under pressure, the better golfer could choose.

The set up

With the ball sitting well, i.e. with a cushion of grass beneath it, use a sand wedge and set up with the club face square,

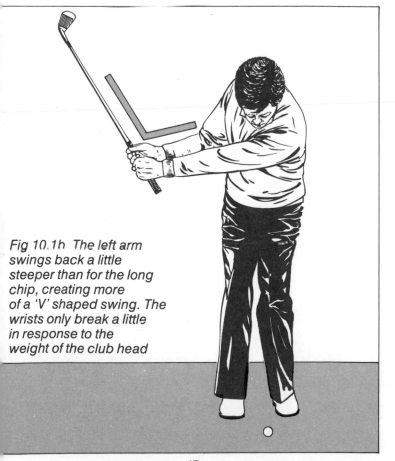

Fig 10.1h The left arm swings back a little steeper than for the long chip, creating more of a 'V' shaped swing. The wrists only break a little in response to the weight of the club head

gripping nearer the end of the club than for the chip shot. The stance should be narrow and open, i.e. aimed left of the target, but the shoulders parallel to the target. Ensure that you bend forward from the hips so that your arms have room in which to swing, and your weight is towards the balls of your feet. The back of the ball should be positioned just inside the left heel, with the hands ahead of the ball so that the shaft and left arm form a straight line. The ball is not as far back in the stance as for the chip shot, and so more effective loft faced on the club will be used. The weight should slightly favour the left side (Fig 10.1a).

The swing

Swing the left arm away more steeply than for the chip shot, and you will find that the wrists will cock naturally a little under the swinging weight of the club head, but do not make any conscious effort to break them (Fig 10.1b). Some of your weight will transfer to the right leg, and then as the left arm swings the club *down* and through, just feel that you are pulling the club head through the ball with no conscious strike. At the same time, the weight transfers

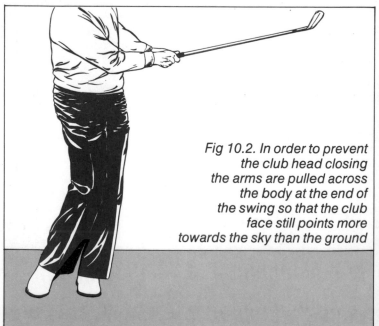

Fig 10.2. In order to prevent the club head closing the arms are pulled across the body at the end of the swing so that the club face still points more towards the sky than the ground

Fig 10.3. In the more advanced short pitch shot, the wrists actively cock early in the backswing so that the angle between the shaft and arms is greater than for the easier pitching method. This creates a steep narrow arc with little shoulder turn, and the club shaft is almost vertical

back to the left leg, which not only gives some rhythm to the shot, but enables you to swing through without closing the club face. It is important to keep the back of the left hand firm. When you finish, the face of the club and the back of the left hand should be looking more towards the sky than the ground, and your hands and arms will have been pulled across your body (Fig 10.2). The swing is not dissimilar to that of the long chip, although the shape of it is more of a 'V' than a 'U'. The club head swings slightly to the inside on the backswing, so that it can approach the ball from the inside and swing straight through to the target.

Although this particular pitching action does not provide the steepest attack or maximum height on the ball, none the less, it is a good way to play those delicate shots around the green, especially when under pressure. If you have to carry a bunker with little green to work with, you may not get as close as you would like, but at least you will be on the green. So if you have trouble pitching, no matter what your handicap, use a firmer and more passive handed action, and your consistency will improve.

The more advanced short pitch

For this example, we will assume that the ball is sitting reasonably well on a cushion of grass. This will enable you to use a sand wedge, the most lofted club in the bag, and ideal for the shot. With the same set up as above, in the backswing, you should swing your arms up steeply, feeling that your wrists cock quite early, creating a steep narrow arc. Where many people go wrong is that they initiate the backswing with their hands alone. Instead, you must swing the arms up, and cock the wrists as well, creating a 'V' shaped swing where the shaft is almost vertical at the top of the swing (Fig 10.3). There is minimal shoulder turn and not much weight transference, with the head remaining quite still. From the top of the swing, the left arm pulls down, and the club head slides under the ball as the knees move towards the target. In this method of pitching, you will feel that your hands are more active through impact, with the right hand working under the left, and never crossing over it. You will also cut across the ball a little from out to in, due to

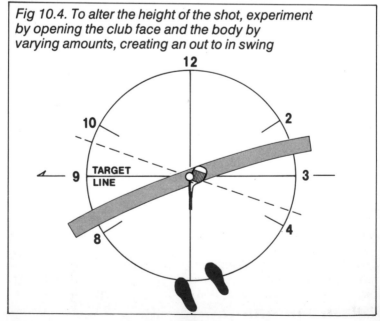

Fig 10.4. To alter the height of the shot, experiment by opening the club face and the body by varying amounts, creating an out to in swing

the extra wrist action and lack of shoulder turn. The finish is the same as for the more passive handed shot, with the arms drawn very much across the body. When the ball is not sitting on a good cushion of grass, you will have to think of hitting down more, rather than sliding the club under the ball, and perhaps playing it marginally further back in the stance.

In each of these methods, the left arm must swing through the ball, not just at it, and the head must remain anchored until the ball is on its way, as any temptation to look up too soon can be disastrous.

How to vary the shot

There are many combinations that can be applied to this shot, whether you use the passive or active handed technique, and each situation may demand something different. Practise first as described above with a square club face and shoulders parallel to the target so that you can learn how high your particular action and sand wedge will hit the ball.

Then open the club face, i.e. turn it to the right before gripping it, thus adding loft to the club, and aim yourself left of target. In doing this, you align your body and thus the swing line more in the 2 to 8 o'clock direction, so that you create a slicing action across the ball in relation to the target (Fig 10.4). The actual swing is just the same, but because you have set up left of target it thereby creates a steep out to in swing which, combined with the open clubface, will send the ball much higher and it will not roll very far on landing. However, a word of warning about this shot: when you open the sand iron, you bring the flange into play which tends to bounce off the ground. So really you can open the club face only when you have enough grass under the ball, thereby allowing the flange to slide beneath it. You can always open the wedge, which has no flange, and play the same shot, but the ball will not fly so high. The amount that you open the club face and your body will alter the height and length of the shot, so you do need to be aware of the effect of these adjustments in order that the power of your swing is correct.

Spend some time practising from bad lies as well as good, so that when faced with the same shot on the course, you will know what to expect and approach the whole situation in a calm manner.

CHAPTER 11

The long pitch

This is the shot that sometimes draws gasps of admiration from the galleries as the ball lands and then spins backwards. However, many golfers fail to appreciate that you can only make the ball behave in such a fashion under certain circumstances. First, the ball must be lying well with no grass behind it, so that the face of the club can contact the ball cleanly; secondly, the shot must be hit quite hard, and

Fig 11.1a. The stance should be open and reasonably narrow, with the feet just angled towards the target and the weight on the outside of the left and inside of the right foot. The hands are ahead of the ball with the left arm and shaft in a straight line

therefore you must be an adequate distance from the green; thirdly, the green must be receptive, i.e. fairly soft, or sloping towards the player. In Great Britain, the greens tend to be on the firm side in summer, and so to be able to spin the ball backwards is quite difficult, if not impossible.

Fig 11.1b. At the top of the swing the wrists are fully cocked with the last three fingers gripping firmly. Through impact the hands stay well ahead of the ball with the left resisting the power of the right

However, it would be wrong to let the spectacular element of the shot overshadow its real purpose, i.e. to send the ball to the green, mainly through the air, so that when it lands it runs a minimum distance.

The set up

Although we use a full backswing for a long pitch, it is still a fairly narrow arc so that the club head descends quite steeply onto the ball. To get the correct amount of resistance in the backswing, the feet are set open to the target, i.e. aimed left, are not too wide apart and are angled slightly towards the target with the weight favouring the outside of the left, and the inside of the right, foot (Fig 11.1a). The shoulders are parallel to the target line so that the line of the swing is inside-straight-inside. The ball is about three inches inside the left heel, hands ahead of the ball, with the shaft and left arm forming a straight line.

The swing

The left arm swings the clubhead away on a relatively steep arc, and quite early in the backswing the wrists will be fully cocked. Since this is a long shot, you are not so likely to fall into the trap of starting the backswing with the hands, but do make certain that it is your arms that get the club head moving initially. At the top of the swing, your shoulders will turn, although not as much as for a drive; the weight will transfer to the inside of the right foot, but the left heel should not leave the ground, since you want to build up a resistance between your legs and the top half of the body (Fig 11.1b). The last three fingers of your left hand should grip the end of the club firmly, as there is considerable pressure at this point with the wrists fully cocked.

As the downswing starts, the weight transfers back to the left leg, and the left arm *pulls* the club head *down* towards the ball. At impact the wrists straighten but the hands are ahead of the ball, just as they were at address. There is a definite strike with the hands to give added crispness and to help create the backspin. Do *not* let the left wrist buckle under the power of the right hand, but keep the back of the hand moving towards the target (Fig 11.1b). The follow through is somewhat curtailed so that the shot is punched away with a good divot being taken after striking the ball.

How to vary the height of the shot

If you want to play a pitch shot with less height, position the
ball further back in the stance towards the right foot, thus
the club hooding at address, and therefore subtracting
effective loft from it. Keep a little more weight on the left leg

*Fig 11.2. This shows the feet and ball position, and swing
path for the normal, low and high pitch shots*

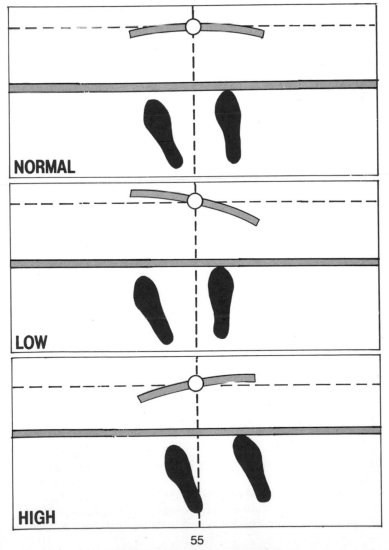

than for the standard pitch shot, with the hands well ahead of the ball. As the ball is played back in the stance, contact is made whilst the clubhead is still swinging from inside the target line, rather than straight towards the target. Therefore, there is a tendency for this shot to fly a little right of target (Fig 11.2). Allow for this either by aiming just left of target, or closing the clubface – the second option will take more loft off the club and hit the ball lower. As with the standard pitch, swing the arms steeply in the backswing, then hit down on the ball, with a good release of the hands at impact. Keep the left wrist very firm – to promote the punch element in the shot and abbreviate the follow through.

If you have a tall tree to play over, you may need extra height to the shot, and in this instance you should play the ball a little further forward in the stance, i.e. nearer the left foot than normal (Fig 11.2). I should add that if the lie is awful, you will find this shot very difficult and may have to consider another route to the hole. Ideally, you do need some grass under the ball. So with the ball forward, open your stance and your shoulder line so that they aim left of target, creating a steep out to in swing path (Fig 10.4). Depending on how high the ball needs to go, you can open the blade of your wedge, or sand wedge, so that it aims right of target. Keep your hands about level with the ball so that the shaft is vertical rather than sloping towards the target and your weight evenly distributed or, if you have a very good lie, slightly favouring the right side. This set up will enable you to swing the club back with the hands and arms, cocking the wrists early in the backswing. You must not allow the club face to close through impact, and so the knees must move towards the target as the arms swing down and you finish with the club face pointing more towards the sky. What you must remember with this shot is that most of the force will be sending the ball upwards, and not forwards, so it is good practice to find out how far the ball goes when you hit it as high as you can. You need to be able to carry the depth of a large tree as well as its highest branches.

How far should you hit a pitch shot?

When you are using the higher numbered clubs, you should be concentrating mainly on accuracy, and not length from the club. It is no use thrashing your wedge an extra ten yards if 50 per cent of the time you miss the green. You can play a pitch shot best with the 8 iron to sand wedge, so find out how far you hit each club, and also how far the ball goes before it lands. Your 9 iron may cover a total distance of 120 yards, but it may only carry 110 yards. As you will probably wish to carry bunkers with short shots, it is therefore vital to know the carry with each club. On the practice ground, hit about fifteen shots with each club, note the average distance, and for safety's sake assume that the carry is ten yards less with each club. Your accuracy will improve when you hit the short irons at about 80 per cent of your maximum effort. It is far better to learn how to hit a three-quarter 9 iron than to slog away with the wedge. You can always grip down on a less lofted club and make your normal swing, more in control of yourself and the ball.

Fig 11.3. By trying to force a wedge shot you can easily mis-hit it. Better to play a controlled 9 iron that easily carries the bunker. If you hit your 9 iron comfortably 120 yards, for safety's sake, assume that the ball will land about 10 yards short of the total distance and roll the rest. Do not be afraid to hit beyond the pin; the ball will stand a chance of going in, and 5 or 10 yards past is just as near as 5 or 10 yards short. The only time to be less aggressive is if you wish to leave yourself an uphill putt, or the hole is cut very close to the back of the green

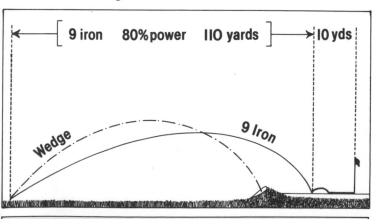

CHAPTER 12

Bunkers need not become a hazard

Despite what many golfers think, to get out of the average bunker is not the most difficult shot in golf. The technique for escaping from these sand hazards – the splash shot – has to be learnt. Once mastered, the fear of bunkers that haunts the golfer who lacks the correct technique, will disappear and his/her results will improve dramatically. There is a tendency to rush the shots you fear, and I see so many players who dart into a bunker, take a short sharp jab at the ball and have to repeat this action three or four times before they manage to get the ball out. It is not difficult to get out of most bunkers. Admittedly, some are easier than others, but becoming accurate with bunker shots takes time and practice, which few club golfers ever devote to bunker play. Unfortunately, many clubs do not have a practice bunker, but you can usually hit a couple of extra shots at some point on the course when it is quiet. Before discussing technique, I would like to explain briefly about sand wedges.

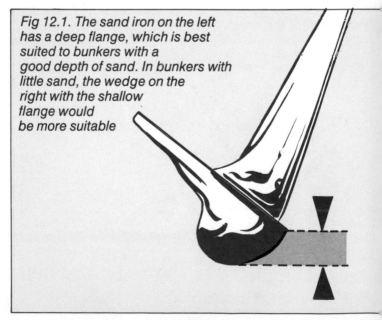

Fig 12.1. The sand iron on the left has a deep flange, which is best suited to bunkers with a good depth of sand. In bunkers with little sand, the wedge on the right with the shallow flange would be more suitable

The right equipment

To make bunker shots easier, the sand wedge is the best club to use. Apart from being the most lofted club in the bag, it has what is called a flange on its sole, which is lower than the leading edge of the club and is designed to bounce on the sand and stop the club head digging in too deeply. When the blade is turned open, this flange comes more into play and the leading edge sits further off the ground. If you do not own a sand wedge, you can use the pitching wedge, which is more inclined to dig into the sand and is not as lofted as a sand wedge. The size and depth of the flange varies from club to club and, depending on the type of sand your bunkers possess, one type of club will be more suitable. If there is not much sand, you want a club with a shallow flange that will not bounce off the harder surface, whereas for bunkers with deep powdery sand, a deeper flange will prevent the club going too far under the ball (Fig 12.1). Many professionals carry a selection of clubs so that they can use the one that best suits the conditions at each course. You cannot go to that extreme, but ask your professional whether the club in your set is best for you and your course.

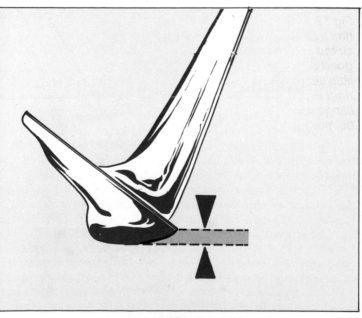

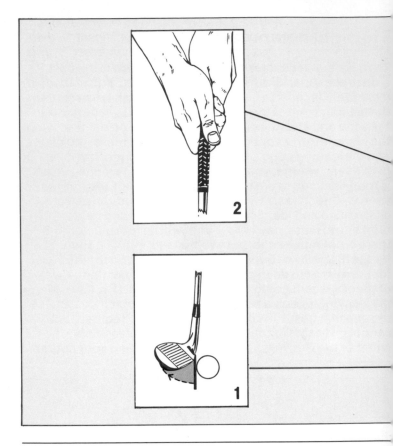

The grip and set up for the splash shot

The first thing to do is to turn the club face open a little so that it faces right of the target, which makes the flange more effective and also adds loft to the club. What you must do, however, is to spin the club open and then take your grip, so that it will remain in this position when you strike the ball (Fig 12.2). It is a good idea to grip down on the club for added control, and since you will incur a penalty if the club head touches the sand prior to impact, you may find it prudent to take your grip outside the bunker. Your normal grip is perfectly suitable, although someone with a strong grip might get better results either by opening the club quite a lot, or turning the hands a little more to the left on the grip.

To offset the open club face, and to promote a steep out to in swing, you must now align yourself left of the target so

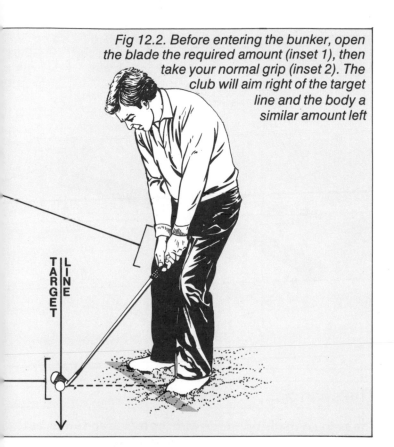

Fig 12.2. Before entering the bunker, open the blade the required amount (inset 1), then take your normal grip (inset 2). The club will aim right of the target line and the body a similar amount left

TARGET LINE

that a club placed across your shoulders would not be parallel to the target, but aimed possibly three or four yards left, depending on the particular shot in hand (Fig 12.2). So using the clock face analogy, with the target still at 9 o'clock, your shoulders and body will be lined up more towards the 2 to 8 o'clock line with your feet a little open to that, and consequently your swing will also be more in the 2 to 8 o'clock direction (Fig 12.3). The stance is fairly narrow with the weight favouring the left foot. When taking your stance you must wriggle your feet into the sand so that your stance is secure, and in doing this you can, quite legitimately, learn something about the texture of the sand and how deep it is. The ball is played opposite the left instep, but since you are not trying to hit the ball, but the sand behind it, look at a spot about two inches behind the ball, and hold the club just above this point. Remember that you must not let the club head touch the sand until impact.

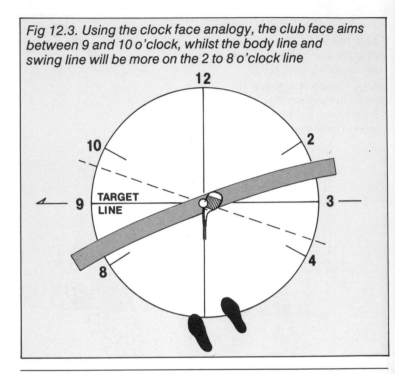

Fig 12.3. Using the clock face analogy, the club face aims between 9 and 10 o'clock, whilst the body line and swing line will be more on the 2 to 8 o'clock line

The swing

The swing is made primarily with the hands and arms, but make certain that you do not just pick up the club with your hands and chop at the ball. In an effort to swing from out to in, some golfers feel that they should quickly raise their hands and swing their arms significantly away from the body on the backswing. By setting up as I have just described so that your body is open to the target, you have pre-selected the line of the swing, which is automatically out to in (Fig 12.4). So just swing your arms up in the backswing allowing your wrists to cock, but do not push your arms away from your body. There is little shoulder turn or weight transference. Swing your arms down and, with your hands leading the club head, enter the sand at the predetermined spot behind the ball. At the same time, just as in the short pitch shot, your legs must be active. Transfer the weight more onto the left side ensuring that your knees slide towards the target. Hit right through the sand so that the club head removes a shallow divot of sand about six inches long, on which the ball is sitting. The club face must

Fig 12.4. This clearly shows how the set up has dictated that the swing path is out to in. With little shoulder turn, the arms and hands have swung the club head on a steep arc with little weight transference

not close through impact and should be facing more towards the sky at the completion of the shot (Fig 12.5). Again, as with most shots in the short game, the left hand must not be overpowered by the right, but must stay firmly in control throughout. In the follow through, the arms are drawn very much across the body.

Through and just after impact, you must keep your eye firmly fixed on the sand, resisting any temptation to see the results of your efforts too soon. Just because you are not hitting the ball very far, do not imagine that you should take a very short backswing. Sand provides a great resistance to

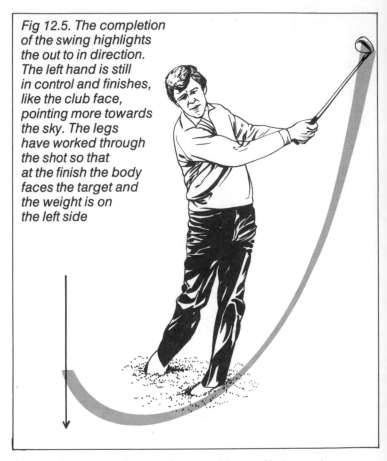

Fig 12.5. The completion of the swing highlights the out to in direction. The left hand is still in control and finishes, like the club face, pointing more towards the sky. The legs have worked through the shot so that at the finish the body faces the target and the weight is on the left side

the club head, and it must be travelling sufficiently fast when it enters it to create enough momentum to move through the sand. Women golfers often have more problems with bunkers, simply because they will not take a long enough backswing; the club just dies in the sand and the ball goes nowhere. So take a full backswing, just using your arms and hands, and be certain to swing right through so that at the finish you are facing your target, much as you would be on a shot from the fairway. In fact, the splash shot resembles a short pitch shot, but it is aimed left of the pin, hitting the sand and not the ball.

The best bunker players give the impression that the whole swing is rather lazy and languid, almost as though it was in slow motion. Try to imitate them, and make your swing long and lazy rather than short and stabbing.

Remember that you are trying to remove the sand around and under the ball from the bunker, and the ball will go with it (Fig 12.6). At first, you should consider success as being able to get the ball out of the bunker each time with your first shot, not worrying too much about the length but concentrating on making a rhythmical swing right through the ball so that it goes virtually towards the pin, even if it finishes short or runs past it.

Bunker practice

Like all shots in golf, you need club head control, and to test this, and indeed to improve it, draw a straight line in the sand representing the spot at which you want the club head to enter it. Then swing without the ball, trying to hit that line. Until you can do this reasonably efficiently, your bunker play will be inconsistent.

To help you appreciate how to align both yourself and the club face at address, draw a line through your ball towards the pin. This represents the 3 to 9 o'clock line in the clock face analogy, and it will enable you to see that the open clubface will point between 9 and 10 o'clock, whilst your body and swing line are along 2 to 8 o'clock.

To give you a mental picture of what you are trying to do, imagine that the ball is sitting on a five pound note or a dollar bill. You are trying to remove all the sand beneath the note from the bunker, and inevitably the ball will go with it.

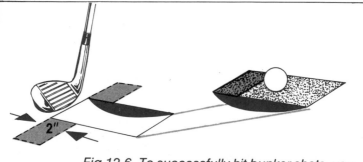

Fig 12.6. To successfully hit bunker shots, you must remove from the bunker the sand on which the ball is sitting. The club head enters about two inches behind the ball and removes a shallow divot about six inches long in the middle of which is the ball

CHAPTER 13

Varying the length of a bunker shot

Having practised the basic bunker shot so that you can at least get the ball out of the bunker, you will want to refine this skill in order to vary the length for accuracy. There are a number of ways of doing this and I will outline three different systems.

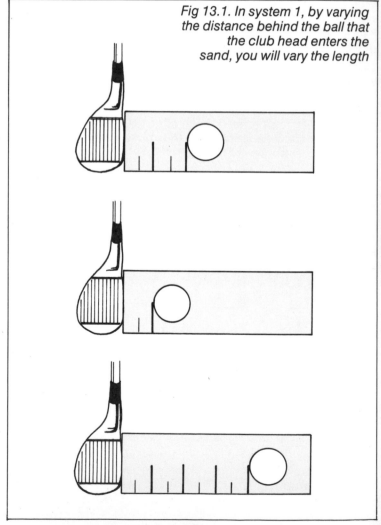

Fig 13.1. In system 1, by varying the distance behind the ball that the club head enters the sand, you will vary the length

System 1

In the previous chapter I suggested that the clubhead should enter the sand two inches behind the ball. If you retain the same set up but vary this distance, keeping the same strength swing, you are altering the amount of sand between the club face and ball, and thus altering the power of the shot. The weakness of this system is that you must be well in control of the club head so that you can hit the sand at exactly the right spot. You must also take care that on the really short shots where you are entering the sand perhaps four inches behind the ball, you can still swing through the sand (Fig 13.1).

System 2

By keeping the strength of swing and point of entry the same, but varying the amount that the club face is opened and with it the amount you aim to the left, the power is altered. With the blade opened, so that it is aimed about 45 degrees right of target and your body the same amount left, you will produce a pronounced out to in slicing action across the ball with a very lofted club. In this instance, the ball will go high and not very far; therefore, by varying these two elements of the shot, you can alter the length and height achieved. One of the weaknesses of this system is that a very open club face on firm sand is not easy to use, and the player may find it difficult to get the angles right (Fig 13.2).

System 3

By keeping the amount the club face and body are turned open and the point of entry the same, you can vary the distance by how hard you hit the shot. This means that there is only one variable, and it would seem therefore to be the easier system to use, since you just have to work on how far back to swing the club, much as you would with a short pitch shot. The weakness of this system is that on very short shots there is a possibility that you could not swing the club head slowly enough for the correct distance, and still keep it moving through the sand. There is also a limit to how far you could hit the ball. However, once you have mastered the idea that you have to swing through the ball, and not just

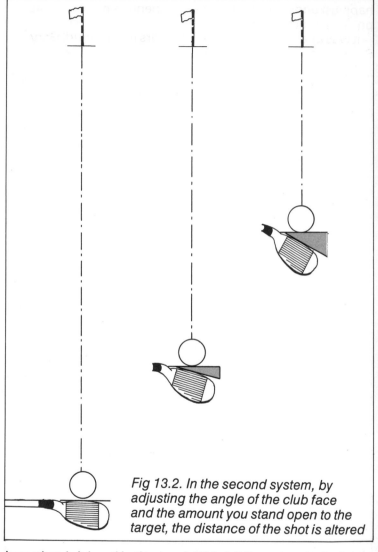

Fig 13.2. In the second system, by adjusting the angle of the club face and the amount you stand open to the target, the distance of the shot is altered

bury the club head in the sand, I think this system is the best because it has only one variable, i.e. the amount of effort in the swing. When its limits have been reached, you have to adjust the club face and body line accordingly, but for the majority of shots, a constant set up and entry point can be maintained (Fig 13.3).

Each system has its weaknesses and strengths, and the best bunker players are able to use a combination of all three. You must choose the system with which you feel happiest and most confident, and spend as much time as possible practising different shots.

It was one of the best bunker players in the world, Gary Player, who said, 'The more I practise, the luckier I get'.

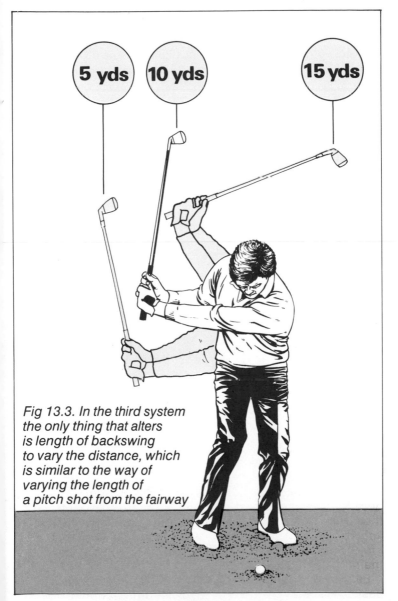

Fig 13.3. In the third system the only thing that alters is length of backswing to vary the distance, which is similar to the way of varying the length of a pitch shot from the fairway

CHAPTER 14

Imperfect lies

The plugged ball

Playing a plugged ball out of a bunker is not as difficult as it may seem. The main problem with the shot is trying to control the ball, which will run much more than a shot from a decent lie. In the splash shot from the bunker, the club face was opened to increase the effectiveness of the flange, thus preventing the club head from going too deep into the sand. However, when a ball is plugged, it sits lower in the sand, and your challenge is to hit deep enough to get the club head below it. Consequently, by opening the club face, you would make the shot more difficult. Therefore, keep it square or a little closed at address. You also square up the shoulder line, but keep the stance narrow and a little open and wriggle your feet deeper into the sand than normal. The ball is played back in the stance near the right foot, and there is more weight on the left leg than the right.

Fig 14.1. When the ball is plugged, play it back in the stance near the right foot, with the weight more on the left foot. Keep the blade square, then swing your arms up steeply, hitting the sand about an inch behind the ball

From this set up, you can easily create a steep angle of attack on the ball, which will remove it readily from the bunker. Swing your arms almost straight up from the ball and concentrate on hitting the sand about one inch behind it. Most of your effort will be downward, and although you must not quit on the shot, the follow through will be curtailed. The ball will come out lower than usual and run, and therefore you should take this into account when deciding on how and where to play the shot (Fig 14.1).

Hard sand

If the ball sits on hard, or firmly packed, wet sand, it will be more difficult for the club head to penetrate the sand, and the flange can be inclined to bounce off it, making it easy to thin the shot. To offset this, play the ball nearer the middle of the stance and aim to hit the sand about one inch behind the ball, concentrating on hitting down through the shot. I would recommend that in very firm sand you keep the club face square, as in the plugged ball shot, so that the flange does not really come into play. Alternatively, you could consider using a wedge, which has a sharper leading edge and will penetrate the sand more easily (Fig 14.2).

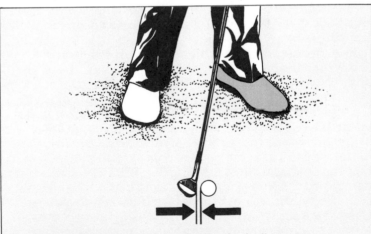

*Fig 14.2. In hard packed sand, play the ball nearer
the centre of the stance than for the normal
splash shot. If the sand is very firm, also
square the blade. Try to hit the sand
closer to the ball than normal, concentrating
on hitting down through the shot*

CHAPTER 15

Long bunker shots

The over-riding point to consider with these shots is the angle at which the ball will leave the bunker. It is easy to be over-ambitious and take too much club, resulting in the ball not clearing the bunker face. I would recommend that you position the ball a little nearer the centre of your stance to give yourself a better chance of hitting the ball first, but bear in mind that this will reduce the effective loft on the club. It would be better always to err on the side of caution, and take one less club, i.e. a 7 instead of a 6, and have the knowledge and confidence that you have enough loft to get the ball out of the bunker safely. I always like to open the club face just a touch so that I have some extra loft on my side.

Take your normal stance and set up for the iron in question, and only just wriggle your feet into the sand so that you have a firm base (Fig 15.1). You can align your body parallel to the target, and make a normal inside-straight 4 to 9 o'clock swing. Grip down the club a little with firm rather than light pressure, which will help to eliminate excessive wrist action. Do not transfer too much weight in the backswing; feel that just your arms and hands swing the club back. The downswing should be like a normal shot from the fairway, where the legs just lead the arms. If your legs do not play their part, the club will probably hit the sand first. When the ball is sitting on top of the sand, you will be able to sweep it away, just taking a shallow divot of sand after the ball, and in this instance it is helpful to look at the top, rather than the back, of the ball as this will encourage you to hit it cleanly. Should the ball be lying down even slightly, then you must make a steeper attack on it, trying to hit as close to it as possible. You could set up a little open so that you create an out to in swing (Fig 15.2). The shot will be dampened to some extent by the sand behind the ball, but providing you have not been too ambitious with club selection, it should still come out a reasonable distance. Always swing easily on these shots as any sudden movements can cause you to lose your footing and balance.

Those shots around the green of about 40–50 yards are perhaps the hardest to judge, even for the best players in the world. If you have decided to hit the ball cleanly, then even a few grains of sand can ruin your plans. In firm sand from this distance, it may be worth playing a wedge or a 9 iron and

Fig 15.1. For long shots from bunkers, take your normal stance for the club being used and grip more firmly, and further down the club than usual, to help eliminate excessive wrist action. Play the ball nearer the centre of the stance, and looking at the top of the ball, try to sweep it off the top, taking a shallow divot of sand after the ball

hitting just behind the ball, allowing for the sand the take power from the shot.

For the really long shot, providing the bunker is shallow, you will find that a fairway wood, such as a 5 or 7 wood, is the best to play. These clubs have more loft than a 3 or 4 iron and have a tendency to bounce across the sand rather than dig in. Grip down the club as before, and place the ball nearer the centre of the stance than normal. Position the body parallel to the target so that the line of the swing is from inside to straight, i.e. 4 to 9 o'clock, and then try to sweep the ball off the top of the sand. The swing may feel wooden, since there will be little wrist action, but keep it smooth and unhurried and the ball will go a long way. Do not be tempted to thrash it; instead, play it like a three-quarter shot.

As with any shot in golf, this must be practised so that you know how much club you can risk. Unfortunately, if long bunker shots are not successful, they can prove rather costly and then you will wish that you had been more cautious.

Fig 15.2. If the ball sits down a little in the sand, set up with an open stance and club face. This will give you a steeper out to in swing which will fade the ball out of the bunker

CHAPTER SIXTEEN

Putting it to work

The previous chapters of this book have detailed in some length a variety of shots played from about 100 yards in. However, no amount of words or tuition will improve your short game to its maximum standard, unless *you* work on this department yourself. Once you have played golf for some time, it will be relatively easy to hit the ball, say, 140 yards; you simply take the appropriate club for the shot. To teach someone to hit the ball 30 or 40 yards for instance, either as a putt, chip, pitch or from a bunker, is more difficult. You do not have a club that is designed by the manufacturers to hit the ball 30 yards, and so you must create a swing that will hit the ball the required distance. Your task is further complicated by the fact that you may need to hit the ball high or low, which means using different clubs for each shot, and consequently differing amounts of power in the swing.

A professional can give you the correct technique for any of the short game shots and, as I have done, explain how to develop a knowledge of how the ball reacts with different clubs. But only by practising will you be able to recall readily which is the correct club and correct strength swing for the different situations that you will encounter during your golfing life. Over a period of time you will build up a casebook history of shots that you can instantly call on, based upon experience and practice. In each of the four main departments of the short game, i.e. putting, chipping, pitching and bunkers, you will seldom use your full power to play any shot. Instead, a combination of club selection and distance must dictate how hard to hit the ball. You should view the development and improvement of your short game in five sections.

1 Perfecting the strike

Until such time as you can strike the ball out of the middle of your club, whether it is your putter, wedge or sand iron, you will not be able to advance as quickly as you could. The beauty about the short game, however, is that you can practise it in very little space, both indoors and outside. You can putt and chip indoors on the carpet, although it may be best to chip off a spare piece of carpet if you have one. You can also chip and pitch from a coconut mat in your garden, which will save taking divots from the lawn (Fig 16.1). The fact that the ball is not landing on a green will not prevent you from improving your strike, or developing a sense of distance for shots. You can try to land the ball at specific targets, perhaps five yards apart. Most clubs have an area where you can practise these shorter shots, even if they do not have a large practice ground.

Fig 16.1. By practising in your garden hitting balls from a coconut mat to specific targets, you can quickly improve the quality of strike and your judgement of distance

2 Visualization

I am sure that this is an aspect of golf that is most under-used by the majority of club golfers. Instead of developing this sense, so often they take any club from the bag and knock the ball forwards towards the hole without any real preconceived idea of where to land the ball, or how hard to swing. Professionals visualize every shot before they play it, and no department of golf demands this ability more than the short game, where often several alternative shots are possible. You should always try to imagine where the ball must land, how it will roll and then 'see' it going into the hole. You may like to play some shots, allowing the ball to run over contours in the green, or, alternatively, you may prefer to fly the ball over any slight undulations to be assured of a more predictable bounce (Fig 16.2). Start to think about holing shots around the green, even if in reality it may seem an unlikely outcome. By being more positive, you may be pleasantly surprised at just how close you can get to holing shots, leaving yourself the shortest of putts. Always try to visualize your playing partners' shots as well, judging how high or low the ball will go, and where it should land and roll if you were playing it. Not only will this advance your progress, but it will help you also to learn about how the course is playing. If you have spent some time practising successfully hitting balls to an umbrella or ball bag, try to imagine yourself back in that situation and transpose your movements to the shot you have to play.

Fig 16.2. There may be more than one way of playing a shot, and you must select the easier and more natural one for you to play

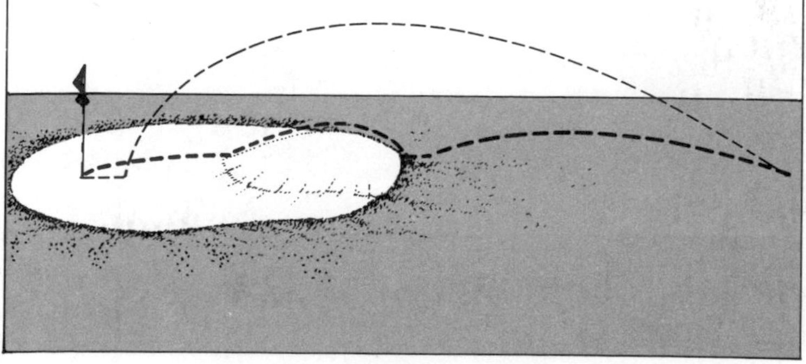

3 Club selection

Having visualized the shot you want to play, you must then select the right club for the shot. If you have a pitch over a bunker without much green between the bunker and the hole, it would be foolish to use a 9 iron. Make life simple and play a wedge or sand wedge (Fig 16.3). Similarly, from just off the green with no hazards between you and the pin some 25 yards away, your sand iron would not be ideal. It would be safer and easier to use a less lofted club, such as a 6 or 7 iron, so that the ball will roll most of the way to the hole. In time you may develop a liking for certain clubs, or get days when you feel happier using one club rather than another, but try to experiment and practise with several different clubs so that your knowledge and repertoire can improve.

Fig 16.3. Always select the correct club for the shot. For a shot that spends more time on the ground than in the air, use a less lofted club.
For a shot that requires height, always choose a more lofted club. Make full use of your set

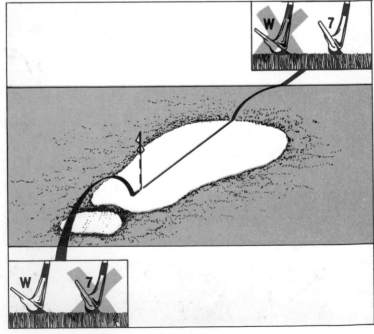

Fig 16.4. Your practice swing should serve to tell you just how hard to hit the ball, and how the entire movement will feel. You should imagine and 'see' the ball going into the hole

4 Rehearsal

Whilst the professionals may have only the briefest of waggles or swings prior to a full shot, for shots that require less than maximum power, they will always have one or two practice swings. This is a serious rehearsal that will convey to the muscles and brain how much force to put into the shot and how their arms, hands, legs and body must feel. At the same time, they will envisage the ball's reaction and 'see' it running up to or into the hole (Fig 16.4). If professionals need this rehearsal, then so do you.

5 Execution

Having prepared properly for the shot, you must now have the courage to go ahead with what you have decided on. It is usually disastrous to change your mind halfway through the shot on how hard to hit it. If you feel that you are under-hitting the shot, the hands suddenly try to add extra power, which more often than not causes a fat or thin shot. Alternatively, if you feel that you are going to hit the ball too far, you will usually decelerate and quit on the spot. So when it comes to the execution of the stroke, aim the clubhead in the correct direction, using an intermediate target about a yard ahead to help you. Take your stance and then just try to repeat your practice swing in an uninhibited and confident manner.

Short game benefits

For the beginner and higher handicap player, short game improvement will radically reduce your scores. Correct technique is relatively simple to understand and to put into operation. It is also easy to practise; you can hit 100 chips, putts or pitches without feeling too exhausted. I have also found that if you are trying to change your grip, the fact that you can hit a lot of shots with little effort will help to make the new grip more familiar and feel more comfortable. You will also develop the correct aim, set up and posture, and eventually clubhead control far quicker, and thus reap the benefit in your long game. Your progress and improvement will ultimately depend on your ability to perfect each of the five sections I have detailed. By becoming more conscious of trying to hole these shorter shots, you will become a more aggressive player. Always try to make a putt finish just past the hole if it does not go in. Better a foot past than an inch short. Do the same with chip shots so that if you do not hole them, the ball finishes two or three feet past the hole rather than short of it. The only time to be more conservative is if going past the hole will leave you an impossible putt back.